Understanding your
Brain

The brains behind this book were:

Rebecca Treays who wrote the words
Christyan Fox who drew the pictures
Professor Nicholas Mackintosh, the Brain expert

and...
Mary Cartwright who did the designs
(with the help of **Russell Punter**)
and **Jane Chisholm** who edited it

INTRODUCTION

CONTENTS

Your brain is just over 1kg (nearly 3lbs) of gooey, slimy, wobbly gelatinous stuff which smells of blue cheese. It sounds revolting, but it is the most vital organ in your body.

The brain rules supreme in the human body. Perched above your neck, beneath your skull, it is the control room which directs almost all your activities: thinking, feeling, talking, moving, and just keeping alive. Without it, you wouldn't really be human at all.

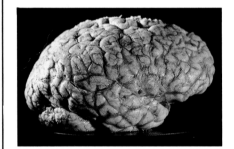

A human brain

Your brain operates 24 hours a day. It never gets tired. It is your own living life-support machine.

> Without your brain you wouldn't be able to do any of the things shown in these pictures.

Taste

Smell

Hear

For links to websites where you can see a real brain, do a 3-D brain puzzle and find lots of brain facts, go to **www.usborne-quicklinks.com**

OLOGISTS

Of course this neuron can receive thousands of signals in one second

Hmm...perhaps it suffered from trauma in its early life.

Different sorts of scientists study the brain in different ways.

Neurologists study the cells in the brain and the nervous system (see page 7).

Psychologists study how humans behave.

Craniologists study the shape and size of the human skull.

Psychiatrists study what happens when the brain goes wrong and people act in strange ways.

Meet Thelma the Thought Bubble. She will help guide you through the amazing world of your brain.

This bump suggests this child has taken part in violent play as part of the process of growing up.

Remember your trip to the beach

Feel overjoyed ...

or under the weather

Have scary nightmares...

Keep your heart beating

Keep breathing

Tell jokes

...or sweet dreams

Keep your balance

3

BRAIN PARTS

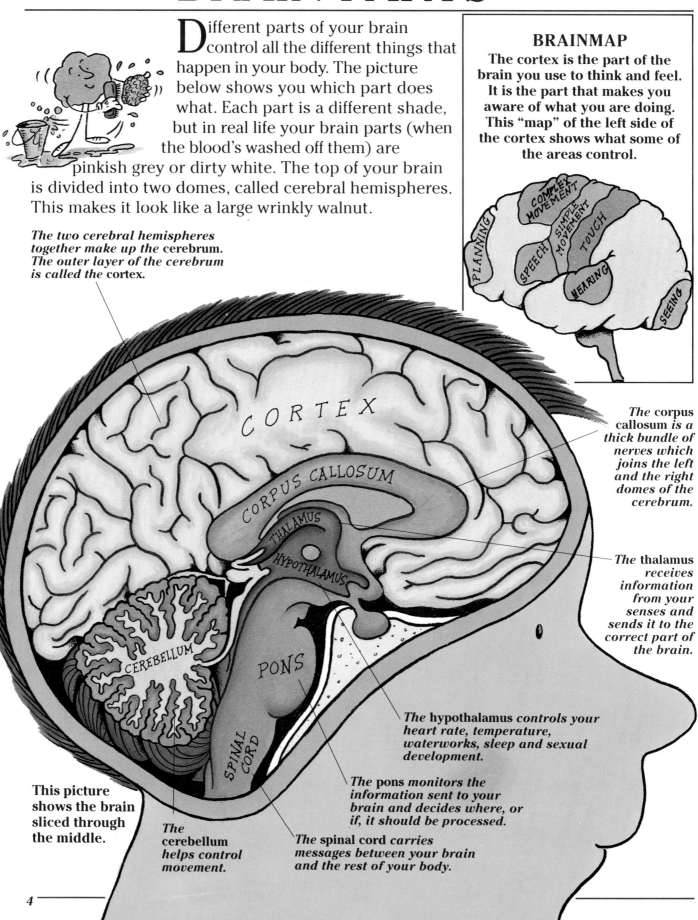

Different parts of your brain control all the different things that happen in your body. The picture below shows you which part does what. Each part is a different shade, but in real life your brain parts (when the blood's washed off them) are pinkish grey or dirty white. The top of your brain is divided into two domes, called cerebral hemispheres. This makes it look like a large wrinkly walnut.

BRAINMAP
The cortex is the part of the brain you use to think and feel. It is the part that makes you aware of what you are doing. This "map" of the left side of the cortex shows what some of the areas control.

PLANNING
COMPLEX MOVEMENT
SIMPLE MOVEMENT
SPEECH
TOUCH
HEARING
SEEING

The two cerebral hemispheres together make up the cerebrum. *The outer layer of the cerebrum is called the* cortex.

CORTEX

CORPUS CALLOSUM

THALAMUS

HYPOTHALAMUS

CEREBELLUM

PONS

SPINAL CORD

The corpus callosum is a thick bundle of nerves which joins the left and the right domes of the cerebrum.

The thalamus receives information from your senses and sends it to the correct part of the brain.

The hypothalamus controls your heart rate, temperature, waterworks, sleep and sexual development.

The pons monitors the information sent to your brain and decides where, or if, it should be processed.

This picture shows the brain sliced through the middle.

The cerebellum helps control movement.

The spinal cord carries messages between your brain and the rest of your body.

HEMISPHERES

Each side of your brain, or cerebral hemisphere, looks after the opposite side of the body. Each side is also in charge of different kinds of thoughts and actions.

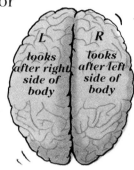

L
looks after right side of body

R
looks after left side of body

The left side is used for speech and language. It is also used for other tasks which require you to do things in a particular order, such as sums or tying a shoelace.

The right side is used for thinking in pictures. If you had to draw a map of the way to school, you would picture the route in your head with the right hemisphere.

Your corpus callosum lets one hemisphere know what the other is doing. Without it, you could read and understand the word "pig" (using your left hemisphere) but would not be able to picture a pig in your mind (which uses the right hemisphere).

RIGHT OR LEFT?

Answer each question and try to figure out which side of your brain it is testing. Solutions on page 32.

1. Which of the boxes a), b), c) or d) can be made by folding the flat piece of paper on the right?

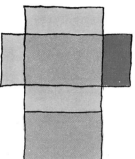

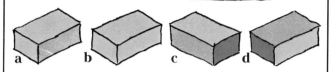

a   b   c   d

2. Which number comes next in the series: 17, 14, 11, 8...(7, 3, 5 or 0)

3. Which is the odd one out?

a   b   c   d   e

4. If Dot goes with Jemma, who does Rosie go with?

Dot   Jemma   Rosie

Anna   Becky   Kathy   or   Mary?

PONS TO THE RESCUE

Have you ever walked into a room where there is a really smelly piece of cheese?

At first, the smell can be completely overwhelming and almost unbearable.

But, after being in the room only a few minutes, you begin to stop noticing it.

The smell hasn't gone, but the pons has stopped sending on the smelly messages to be processed.

WHAT'S INSIDE?

No one understands exactly how the brain works. But scientists know the answer lies with the billions of tiny cells, called neurons or nerve cells, which make up your brain. All your feelings, thoughts and actions are caused by electrical and chemical signals passing from one neuron to the next. It may seem incredible, but a complicated feeling such as jealousy is a series of electrical and chemical changes.

WHAT DOES A NEURON LOOK LIKE?

A neuron looks a little like a tiny octopus, but with many more tentacles (some have several thousand). In all the different parts of your brain, neurons are carrying signals which allow you to move, hear, see, taste, smell, remember, feel and think.

Axon. A larger tentacle, often with branching ends, which carries signals away from the cell body and passes them on to dendrites of other neurons.

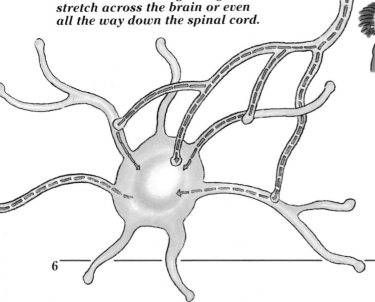

Some axons are long enough to stretch across the brain or even all the way down the spinal cord.

Simple neurons magnified 1000 times

The cell body. Controls the cell and directs all its activites.

Signal passing between neurons.

Dendrites. Tentacles which radiate from the cell body. They receive signals from axons and carry them to the cell body.

HOW DO NEURONS CARRY MESSAGES?

At football games, people sometimes do "The Wave", throwing their arms in the air one after the other. A wave of arms travels from one end of a row to the other. Messages travel down neurons in a similar way. But instead of arms being thrown in the air, tiny pulses of electricity are fired off, one after another, down the length of the axon.

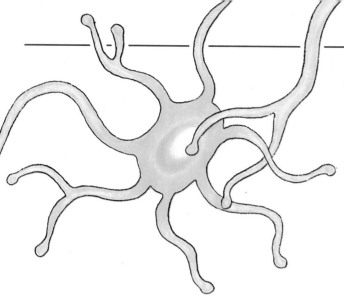

GREY MATTER

Some people say "Use your grey matter" if they want you to think very hard. Grey matter is what makes up most of your cortex. It consists of millions of cell bodies packed tightly together. Much of the rest of the cerebrum is made up of bundles of axons. This is called white matter.

JUMPING THE GAP

Axons and dendrites are separated by tiny gaps called synapses. When a signal reaches the end of an axon, special chemicals are released which spread across the gap. When the chemicals reach the other side, the dendrite fires off an electrical pulse.

THE NERVOUS SYSTEM

The nervous system is a network of neurons stretching from your brain to the tips of your toes. Some neurons send messages to the brain about what's happening inside and outside the body. The brain decides what should be done. Instructions are then sent back down other neurons, via the spinal cord, to muscles, organs or cells, which carry out the response.

If the brain receives information about chocolate cake, it will send a message to your arm to grab it.

STARTLING STATISTICS

• **The fastest brain messages can travel at about 580 kmph (360 mph).**

• **You have about 100 billion neurons. Each one can be connected to thousands of others. This means there are trillions of different routes a message can take around your brain.**

• **Each brain cell may receive hundreds and thousands of incoming signals every second.**

FEEDING THE BRAIN

Your body needs oxygen like a car needs fuel. Oxygen is carried around the body in the blood. Different parts of your body use up different amounts of oxygen, depending on how much they do. The brain is so active it uses almost a quarter of the body's oxygen, although it is only 2% of its total weight.

Pathways of neurons

For links to websites where you can probe a virtual brain, watch a cartoon movie about the nervous system and play games about neurons, go to **www.usborne-quicklinks.com**
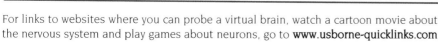

BABY BRAINS

Babies are born with a few, very limited, responses: they can turn their cheek if it is touched, hear and smell, find things to suck, and see black and white patterns. Yet, within only a few days, they can do something as complex as recognizing their mother's face. Their brains have already begun to analyze the outside world. Babies and young children absorb enormous amounts of information every day. You probably learn more in your first five years than in the whole of the rest of your life.

TRIAL AND ERROR

Babies learn by a process of trial and error. As they explore their surroundings, they gradually understand more and more about how the world works.

1. 2. 3. 4.
5. 6. 7. 8.

The picture strip above shows how a baby discovers the link between shaking a rattle and the nice jangly sound it makes.

It takes the baby several chance shakings before he discovers the connection between the rattle and the sound.

These babies are learning as they investigate their world.

BABY TALK

One of the most scientifically baffling things that babies learn to do is to talk.

ma ma!

Between the ages of one and two, a baby learns to utter a few words and to understand simple sentences.

Of course... SUCK...SUCK... NIETZSCHE advanced a doctrine... SUCK...SUCK... of Eternal Recurrence...

Between the ages of two and five, a child learns about ten words a day. (Anyone who has tried to learn a foreign language will know this is an enormous amount.) In three years, a child's vocabulary increases from a few hundred words to as many as 15,000.

Bla-Bla?

OUT OF SIGHT...

The test below was carried out on a nine-month-old baby. It made pyschologists believe that if a young baby couldn't see an object she thought it no longer existed.

The baby is shown a car. She tries to grab it. In full view of the baby, the car is hidden under a cloth. The baby loses interest and doesn't try to get the car.

A later test proved this theory wrong. It showed that a baby does know a thing exists even when she can't see it - but she doesn't think she has any control over it.

The baby tracks a toy elephant moved in front of her face. When the elephant disappears behind a screen, the baby tracks its movements until it reappears. If the elephant is exchanged for a giraffe behind the screen, the baby looks shocked, often bursting into tears. This shows she knew the elephant was still there, even though she could not see it.

HOW THE BRAIN GROWS

Neurologists think that you don't produce any new brain cells after you are born. So brains don't get bigger by adding more neurons. Instead, your brain grows by increasing the number of the connections between neurons. Axons grow new branches which link up with dendrites. As the number of connections between neurons increases, you become capable of more and more complex kinds of thinking.

Any brain cells you lose through a bang on the head can't be replaced. But, with over 100 billion, you can afford to lose a few thousand.

LEARNING TO THINK

As young children, our thinking power is limited. It takes time to understand how the world works.

This child of four agrees that these two beakers hold the same amount of water.

If the water in one beaker is poured into a thinner beaker, in front of the child, she now says the thinner beaker holds more water. A child of seven wouldn't make this mistake.

If this piece of string were straightened out, where would the ends reach: points *a* or points *b*?

Most children under five think the ends would stay in the same place. This is because they cannot yet picture changes in their heads. Most older children know the answer is *b*.

INTELLIGENCE

What makes one person a genius and another just plain average? It is probably a mixture of the brain they are born with and the training they receive. Different people are intelligent in different ways: one may be good at French, but hopeless at chess, while another may understand feelings, but not understand numbers.

BIG HEADS

Some scientists have claimed that big skulls mean bigger brains, and that bigger brains mean brighter people. Men, women and people of different races do have different sized brains. But there is no proof that this has anything to do with how intelligent they are.

TESTING TIMES

In 1905, a Frenchman called Alfred Binet made up some tests to measure intelligence. His tests were meant only to include questions which did not need any special learning. Similar tests, called IQ tests, are still used today. Some people think IQ tests are unfair, because children who are used to doing tests like this usually get higher scores.

BRAIN BOX

Ruth Lawrence was a child genius. At seven, she was taking tests meant for 18-year-olds, and at 11 she was studying at Oxford University. Most of the other students were twice her age.

TAKING THE TEST

IQ tests are made up of different sorts of puzzles and questions. Some use words and numbers, while others use patterns and shapes. This is so that different kinds of intelligence, and both your right and left cerebral hemispheres (see page 4), are tested. Try these tests and see how you do. You can find the answers on page 32.

1. How many triangles are there in this picture? Some smaller triangles may make up bigger triangles.

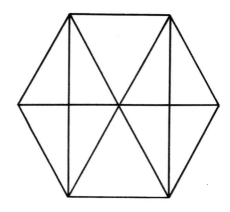

2. Fill in the missing number.

S	H	I	P
19/4	8/15	9/?	16/11
D	O	C	K

3. Which of these shapes will complete the square?

BORN OR BRED?

Inside all your cells are tiny chains of chemicals, called genes. Genes carry instructions which control how your body works. If you were born with a fixed level of intelligence, it would be controlled by your genes.

No two people have exactly the same genes - except for identical twins. If intelligence comes from genes, identical twins should be equally intelligent. This means they should have similar IQs, even if brought up apart.

When psychologists looked at separated twins' IQ tests, they found that they had a high chance of having much the same result. This backs up the argument that at least part of intelligence comes from your genes.

Nick and Paddy are identical twins. They live apart and grew up doing completely different things. See what happened when they both took an IQ test.

4.

4

9

6

? 6 8

Fill in the missing number.

5. Which of the following words means the same as or the opposite of Tall? (Handsome, Dark, Thin, Short, Fat)

6. Beetle/Insect; Sparrow/.... ? (Ant, Dove, Slug, Bird, Feathers).

7.

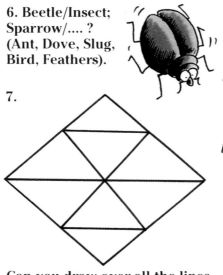

Can you draw over all the lines in this picture without going over any part of a line twice?

8. Which piece from row b makes row a a complete set?

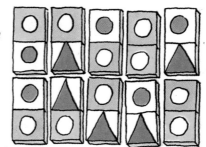

a

b

9. In a box, there are 3 pairs of red boots and 2 pairs of blue boots. How many boots would you have to take out, without seeing them, to be certain of getting a complete pair?

EYESIGHT

Your sense organs receive information from the outside world and turn it into electrical signals. These signals are sent to your brain, where they are interpreted as sights, sounds, smells, tastes and feeling. These two pages show how your eyes and brain work together to let you see.

SEEING

There are three main processes involved in seeing. First, light travels into your eye and a 2-D image is projected onto your retina (which is like a curved screen at the back of your eye). This image is then converted into a series of electrical signals by special cells, called rods and cones. The signals then travel to your brain, where they are interpreted as 3-D images.

Cross-section through an eye.

LENS

RETINA

Brain processes and analyzes electrical pulses and creates a 3-D image.

Optic nerve - bundle of nerves down which electrical pulses travel to the brain.

Flat image of world (known as the retinal image) projected onto retina.

Rods and cones - cells which convert the image on your retina into pulses of electricity.

Real 3-D world

A 3-D WORLD

The image on your retina is 2-D, but you see in 3-D. This is partly because you have two eyes, each of which gives you a slightly different view of an object. These two views are fused by your brain, giving things depth. But your brain also analyzes the retinal image and uses key elements within it to build up a 3-D world in your head.

This picture has the same key elements as the flat image on your retina.

○ *Size. Similar objects of different sizes are interpreted as being at different distances.*

○ *Arrows. Arrow-shaped lines are interpreted as inside or outside corners.*

○ *Overlapping. If one object obscures another, you see the overlapping object as being nearer.*

○ *Lines. Your brain realizes that parallel lines appear to move closer together as they get farther away.*

FUNNY PHOTOS

Because your brain interprets retinal images so quickly, you are not usually aware of their actual size.

In this photo (which is flat like a retinal image) you see two girls. They look the same size, but at different distances from you.

In this photo, the image of the girl who is farther away has been pasted next to the girl in the foreground. She looks much smaller than she did in the photo above.

OPTICAL ILLUSIONS

Optical illusions are the brain making a wrong guess. They tell us how your brain normally analyzes images.

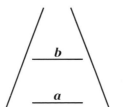

Which line is longer - a or b?

Line *b* looks longer, but *a* and *b* are the same size. Your brain treats the converging lines as parallel, so thinks line *b* is farther away than line *a*. So as lines *a* and *b* project the same-sized retinal images, your brain guesses that line *b* is longer.

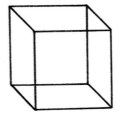

Which face of this cube is at the front?

As you look, the cube seems to flip. You don't have enough elements to work out which way around it is. So your brain makes two guesses, but cannot choose between them.

MORE THAN MEETS THE EYE

Seeing is a lot more than just looking. What you see depends not only on the image on your retina, but also on what you know, expect and want.

12

A   B   C

14

We see the figure in the middle either as the letter B or as the number 13, depending on which way we read the cross.

The pictures in the middle of this series are distorted. Depending on which way you look at the series, you will either see a distorted face or a distorted woman.

BLIND SPOT

The whole of the back of your eye is covered with rods and cones, except for the place where the optic nerve leaves the eye. This tiny spot is called your blind spot. Find your own blind spot by following these instructions.

1. Line up the cross with your left eye. Close your right eye.

2. Look at the cross and move the book slowly away from you.

3. When the book is about a foot away from your eye, the circle disappears.

This is because its image has fallen on to your blind spot. You only notice your blind spot when an object falls on that exact point and nowhere else. Usually your brain just fills in the gap.

MEMORY

L ife without memory would be impossible. You don't just need your memory to recall a telephone number or the date of your best friend's birthday. You need it to remember who you are, how to walk, how to speak and whether or not you like Irish stew. In fact it is your memory that makes you who and what you are.

Everybody has two types of memory: long-term and short-term. Nothing stays in your short-term memory for more than a few minutes. Anything that you can remember for more than that is in your long-term memory. Things can stay in your long-term memory for hours, weeks, months, years or even for the rest of your life.

LONG-TERM MEMORY

Your long-term memory stores everything you know. By the time you are eight years old, it holds more information than a million encyclopedias.

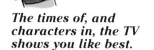

Some of the things in your long-term memory.

DRAGON
SKATEBOARD
GEOGRAPHY

A vocabulary of more than 15,000 words.

How to tie your shoelaces...

and ride a bicycle without falling off.

The times of, and characters in, the TV shows you like best.

JENNY WILLIAM FIZZ
SIMON ANNIE BEN
SALLY SPIKE HARRY

The names of all your class at school.

What you had for dinner last night.

How to find your way home from school.

Who won the World Cup.

How to read, write and add.

This is just the tiniest fraction of what is in your long-term memory. Amazingly, it will never become full, because it has a limitless capacity. This means it could go on storing new information, even if you were to live until you were over a hundred.

SHORT-TERM MEMORY

On the other hand, your short-term memory can only store a maximum of nine things at one time. Most people cannot manage more than seven.

You can test this yourself. Repeat the list of numbers below to several friends. Ask them to write down, in the right order, as many of them as they can remember.

7-9-2-4-1-6-0-5-3-8-6-1-9

Most people can only remember between five and seven numbers.

After a few minutes, facts in your short-term memory are displaced by new ones. The old facts either just fade away or are transferred to your long-term memory.

STORAGE

You store different sorts of information in your memory in different ways. Most facts in your short-term memory are stored as sounds.

Read the first sequence of letters below.

R-J-L-T-M-X-S-Q-F

Write down as many as you can remember in the right order.

Now do the same with the second set of letters.

B-C-T-G-E-P-D-V-G

Most people do better with the first set than the second. This is because in the second set the letters sound similar (bee-cee-tee-etc.), so they get confused more easily.

In your long-term memory, words are usually stored according to what they mean, not what they sound like. If a teacher says "School is closed next week," you would not remember if she had said that particular sentence or another with the same meaning: "Next week, school is shut."

You can also store sights, sounds and smells in your long-term memory. This means you can recognize a famous painting, hum familiar tunes to yourself, and know when your sister's borrowed your mother's perfume.

WHAT ARE MEMORIES?

Everything you learn and all your experiences are encoded in your brain as patterns of electrical pulses passing between neurons.

Memories are patterns of pulses which are repeated without the experience actually taking place. A particular memory returns each time a pattern of electrical pulses is activated.

REMEMBERING

There are some things you never forget, such as your name and age. Other facts and events - such as your worst day at school or your best birthday ever - you can remember whenever you want. But other things can be harder to recall. Remembering can be made easier if you use hints and cues. You can also help yourself by the way you first learn information.

It's easier to remember a fact or event if you are in the place where you first stored it.

Just thinking about the place where you learned something can help too.

Large amounts of information can be very difficult to recall. The way you first learn it can make remembering easier.

Organize the information into groups, and give each one a heading. This is like making a filing cabinet in your head.

When you have to recall the facts, just remembering the headings will make the information easier to recall.

Your memory is full of all sorts of information that, most of the time, you don't even know you have stored.

You would only become aware of it if you were given a strong enough reminder or cue which brings it back to you.

Remembering can be painful. There may be some things that you had hoped to block out of your memory altogether.

For a link to a website where you can play a game to see if you would be a reliable witness, go to www.usborne-quicklinks.com

LOONY LISTS

Imagine you are going shopping tomorrow, and a friend gives you a list of things she wants you to buy for her. You know you are always losing lists, so you want to commit it to memory. If you try learning it by heart, the chances are you will have forgotten a few things by the next day. But if you try to give the list meaning (the sillier the better), you will find it much easier.

One way of doing this is to make all the items on the list part of a story. Another way is to imagine you are walking through your house. As you enter each room you "place" several items in it in strange places or doing funny things.

Items from the shopping list above have been placed in the rooms of this house in rather odd circumstances.

Test this out with a friend. One of you tries to learn the list by heart, by repeating it to yourself. The other uses the placing method. (You could use the house here or your own.) Test yourselves after 24 hours and see who can remember the most.

SHORT-TERM TEST

You can get more in your short-term memory if you can group the facts you have to store into bigger units.

Read over the first set of letters below. Look away and recall as many as you can.

P-S-U-N-E-G-U-F-O-V-I-P-L-A

Now do the same test with the second set.

PS-UN-EG-UFO-VIP-LA

There are 14 items to store in the first set, but in the second, only six.

OVEN MITTS
GLUE
CHOCOLATE MOUSSE
COFFEEPOT
WRAPPING PAPER
BICYCLE
WOOL
BANANAS
SHOES
CAT FOOD
FEATHER DUSTERS

STAYING THE SAME

Whatever you are doing and wherever you are - whether you're sunbathing in Tahiti or skiing in Scandinavia - your brain tries to keep the conditions inside your body the same. The ability to keep the body, and the chemicals inside it, in a stable state is called homeostasis. It is controlled by the tiny part of your brain called the hypothalamus (see page 4).

HORMONES

The hypothalamus triggers the release of hormones into your blood stream. Hormones are chemicals which give instructions to your cells. Some hormones are necessary for homeostasis, while others control your growth and sexual development.

CENTRAL HEATING

Houses with central heating usually work with a thermostat. A thermostat senses how hot or cold it is and automatically turns the radiators on or off, so that the temperature always remains constant.

The hypothalamus is your brain's thermostat. It detects changes in your body temperature, and instructs different parts of your body to heat you up or cool you down as needed.

So even though you feel hotter on a sweltering summer's day than on a icy winter's morning, if you took your temperature it would be the same on both occasions.

If you are getting too hot:

You sweat more because sweating cools down the body.

Your blood flows nearer the surface of the skin so heat can be lost.

Your muscles relax because any movement produces heat.

PHEW!

Hairs lie flat so warm air cannot be trapped next to the skin.

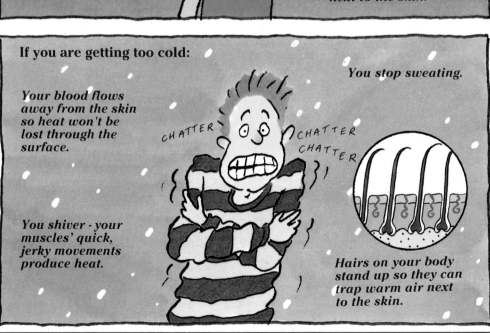

If you are getting too cold:

You stop sweating.

Your blood flows away from the skin so heat won't be lost through the surface.

You shiver - your muscles' quick, jerky movements produce heat.

CHATTER CHATTER CHATTER

Hairs on your body stand up so they can trap warm air next to the skin.

For a link to a website where you can make a model of a brain using your hands, arms, a pencil and a golf ball, go to www.usborne-quicklinks.com

MONITORING THE BLOOD

Your hypothalamus is on 24-hour, around-the-clock blood alert. It is constantly monitoring your blood to make sure it has everything it needs. Here are just some of the things it controls:

OXYGEN UPTAKE

All parts of your body need oxygen to work. Oxygen is carried all over your body by your blood. If you are doing lots of work, such as running up a steep hill, you will need more oxygen than usual. Your hypothalamus will send a message to your lungs telling you to breathe more quickly, so more oxygen from the air can be taken into your lungs and, from there, into your blood.

HUNGER PANGS

You get energy to do things from your food. Food is broken down into sugar and carried in your blood to the busy parts of your body.

RUMBLE... RUMBLE...

If you start to run out of sugar, your hypothalamus makes you feel hungry, so you eat. It also triggers the release of hormones which control how much sugar is taken up by your blood cells. As the sugar level in your blood rises, your hunger pangs disappear.

WATERWORKS AND WASTE

It's very important that your blood contains the right amount of water. With too little, your blood cells would shrivel up, but with too much they would burst.

On its journey around the body, your blood travels through your kidneys. The kidneys are like a filter. Under orders from a hormone triggered by the hypothalamus, they remove from the blood any excess water, along with any nasty waste that has collected. This water and waste make up your urine. If your blood cells need more water, your hypothalamus makes you feel thirsty, so you drink.

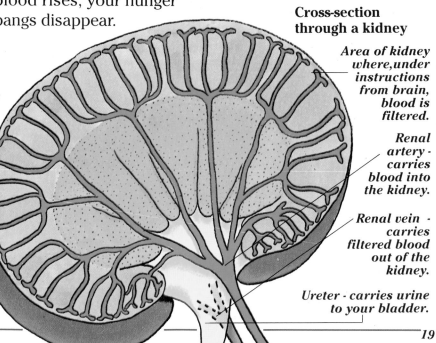

Cross-section through a kidney

Area of kidney where, under instructions from brain, blood is filtered.

Renal artery - carries blood into the kidney.

Renal vein - carries filtered blood out of the kidney.

Ureter - carries urine to your bladder.

CONSCIOUSNESS

Consciousness is what you are aware of at any one moment. It is a constantly changing state. At the moment, you are aware of what you are reading and where you are or maybe of a daydream. But you could switch to something else (what you ate for breakfast, what you plan to do tomorrow) whenever you wanted.

SCREENING

Your brain operates a screening process. Information about what's happening around you is continually entering your brain. But, unless it is considered important (like the sound of your name), it never reaches your conscious mind. This stops your consciousness from getting confused.

Lots of information entering your brain

Information that never reaches your conscious mind

Some of the things that may be hidden in your unconscious

Useful data in your consciousness

RUBBISH

UNCONSCIOUS

Sigmund Freud (1856-1939)

The psychologist Freud believed we also have an unconscious, where we hide embarrassing or painful thoughts. Things in our unconscious come out when we are unaware of what we are doing, for example, in dreams or slips of the tongue.

A FREUDIAN SLIP

Bob borrowed some money from Ted. Ted was livid, but Bob was his friend, so he tried not to think about it. After a few weeks, Ted went to see Bob. "Bob," he said "I've come about your death... I mean your debt". Freud would say Ted unconsciously wanted Bob to die.

SLEEPY HEADS AND DREAMERS

You spend more time sleeping than doing anything else. You are asleep for about one-third of your life - that could be as much as 30 years.

There are two sorts of sleep which are as different from each other as waking is from sleeping. They are called REM (Rapid Eye Movement) sleep and NREM (Non REM) sleep. During REM sleep, your brain is very active.

Activity in the brain is measured by pads, fixed to a person's head, which can pick up electrical pulses in the brain. This is called an EEG (electroencephalograph).

When you are in NREM sleep, you are deeply asleep and hard to wake up. In this state, very little happens in your brain. Throughout the night you switch between NREM and REM sleep. Most people normally fall into NREM sleep at the beginning of the night but, after a couple of hours, they will drift into REM sleep. REM sleep is the time when you dream. The brain becomes as active as when you are awake and your eyes move quickly under your eyelids. This is where the name REM comes from.

EEG readings are recorded as a line called a trace. The closer together on the trace the peaks and troughs are, the more the activity there is taking place.

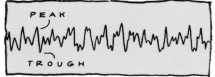

NREM sleep trace - peaks and troughs are far apart

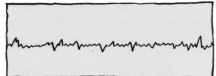

REM sleep trace - peaks and troughs are closer together.

Children dream for about 50% of the night while adults only spend about 20% of the night dreaming.

What do dreams mean and why do we have them? Freud believed that our dreams are about the things in our unconscious. But even in our sleep they cannot be expressed openly, so they are represented as symbols. So, for example, dreaming about setting out on a journey could really be a dream about dying.

Some modern psychologists think REM sleep is the time when the information we have taken in during the day is sorted out. Our memory stores are opened - new information is added to old and new categories are created. As this happens, scraps of memory, old and new, filter briefly into our conscious minds to become dreams.

This boy is dreaming about going hiking. Freud might think he was really dreaming about dying.

MENTAL ILLNESS

Your brain can go wrong, just like any other part of your body. Sometimes this can make you behave abnormally. This is called mental illness. But not all people who behave abnormally are mentally ill. Someone who is very clever is abnormal, but obviously not ill. Mental illness is always distressing and harmful to the sufferer, and to those around them. Two of the most serious forms of mental illness are schizophrenia and depression.

SCHIZOPHRENIA

Delusions of grandeur   **Paranoid delusions**   **Hallucinations**

All schizophrenia sufferers lose control of their own thinking. Some suffer from delusions. This means they believe things that are untrue. A few have delusions of grandeur. This means they think they are powerful and important, or a famous person, such as Jesus. Others have paranoid delusions and believe that people are trying to kill them or that everyone hates them.

Schizophrenics may also have hallucinations. During a hallucination, a person experiences something which isn't really there. Many hear voices telling them to do things (often dangerous) or commenting on their actions.

DEPRESSION

People with depression suffer from deep despair, hopelessness and often complete loss of energy. In some cases this alternates with periods of mania - when they appear to have boundless energy. Although on the surface people in this manic state may appear elated and happy, they are usually not in control and are often frightened and confused.

PHOBIAS

Someone who is afraid of something that most people don't find at all scary is said to have a phobia. Some phobias can seriously interfere with everyday life.

These are some more unusual phobias:

Doraphobia fear of fur

Triskaidekaphobia - fear of thirteen

Arachibutyrophobia - fear of peanut butter sticking to the roof of your mouth

Gymnotophobia - fear of nudity

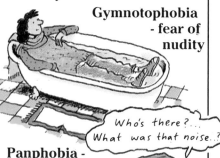

Panphobia - fear of everything

CAUSES AND CURES

Mental illness is probably caused by a combination of abnormalities in the genes you are born with and things that happen in your life (environmental factors). Doctors have two main ways of treating mental illness - biological and psychological treatments.

Biological treatments look at what happens to the chemicals in the brain during mental illness and try to return them to normal.

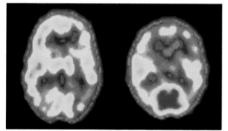

Scan comparing chemical balance of a normal brain (on left) with a schizophrenic brain.

The most common type of biological treatment is with drugs (see page 24).

Psychological treatments, or therapies, try to help people to change the conduct, beliefs and attitudes which are part of their illness, without using drugs. They usually involve the patient getting to know a therapist and working through their problems with him or her. This can take months or years.

STROKES

There are many diseases of the brain which don't cause mental illness.

Strokes, for example, are caused when a blood vessel in the brain bursts or is blocked. The cells around the vessel don't get enough oxygen so they die. Depending on where the blockage occurs, different functions are damaged. People may have problems with speech, movement or memory. One of the oddest defects is when people behave as if they can only see things on their right side, although their eyes are fine. Asked to draw a flower, a patient will only draw the right-hand side.

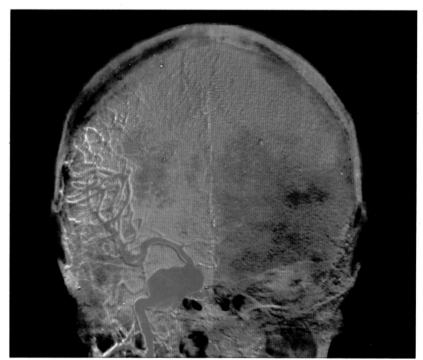

Rear view of the head showing a blockage in an artery on the left-hand side of the brain.

PARKINSON'S DISEASE

Parkinson's disease destroys the neurons that produce a chemical called dopamine. The main part of the brain that is affected by dopamine, is the part that controls movement. Patients often tremble uncontrollably, lose their balance and have problems carrying out the simplest actions like stirring a cup of tea. Drugs relieve the symptoms, but there is no cure.

DRUGS

Drugs change the balance of chemicals in your brain. They are vital in modern medicine and can save lives. But they are also extremely dangerous. They can be addictive (you can't give them up without suffering painful withdrawal symptoms), may change your personality and, if you overdose, they can kill you.

There are four main types of drugs: sedatives, painkillers, hallucinogens and stimulants.

reactions so much that people start slurring their words, become unable to make intelligent decisions and lose their sense of balance.

SEDATIVES

Sedatives slow down the brain, and make you feel sleepy or calm. Doctors often give them to people who are suffering from anxiety. But it's easy to become dependent on these drugs. People begin to think they couldn't cope without them.

Alcohol is a sedative. Small amounts can make people feel relaxed and confident. Larger doses slow down

PAINKILLERS

You've probably taken painkillers, like aspirin, when you've had a headache. Painkillers block the chemicals which make you feel pain. Morphine and heroin are very strong painkillers. They are made from opium, which grows in a kind of poppy. Morphine is given to people in severe pain. Heroin is usually taken illegally. Many users are addicted and go on taking it to avoid painful withdrawal symptoms.

HALLUCINOGENS

Hallucinogens cause hallucinations (see page 22). LSD (also called "acid") is one of the most common illegal hallucinogens. It is taken on small squares of blotting paper which are dissolved on the tongue.

Acid hallucinations may be exhilarating, but they can also be vivid nightmares. Afterward, users often feel upset. Mentally ill people can be particularly seriously damaged.

STIMULANTS

Stimulants speed up activity in your brain and make you feel more alert and sensitive to sights, sounds and feelings. They can help people suffering from severe depression (see page 22). Cocaine and crack are illegal stimulants. They may make users feel good for about 30 minutes, but later they often feel extremely tired and depressed.

OUT OF THIS WORLD?

Have you ever been thinking of someone and only moments later they've phoned you; or had a dream about something that then occurred? Many people believe that incidents like these are the result of mysterious powers of the human brain.

PSI

Psi is what scientists call the unexplained communication of information. It includes extra sensory perception, or ESP, and psychokinesis (the ability to influence events or objects using only mental powers).

There are three types of ESP:

Telepathy - transferring information from one person to another using only thoughts.

Precognition - predicting the future.

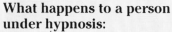

Clairvoyance - being able to perceive things without using your senses.

Believers in psi have tried to set up experiments to prove that it exists. Most scientists remain unconvinced. They think psi has more to do with coincidence than anything else. But many people's own experiences leave them certain that some people have powers that science cannot explain.

HYPNOSIS

Hypnosis used to be thought of as a kind of black magic, which could make people perform amazing feats. Now scientists think hypnosis is a state of extreme suggestibility. Someone under hypnosis will, when commanded by a hypnotist, do things which they would not usually believe they were capable of, but they do not gain super-human powers.

What happens to a person under hypnosis:

She loses her ability to make decisions.

Her attention becomes selective - she will only hear and see what she is told to hear and see.

She may be able to go back in time to experience, for example, her 4th birthday party. Scientists aren't sure if these are true memories or just very vivid imaginings.

When instructed to do so, she can be made to forget what happened during the hypnosis. At a prearranged signal, the memories can be restored.

ANIMAL BRAINS

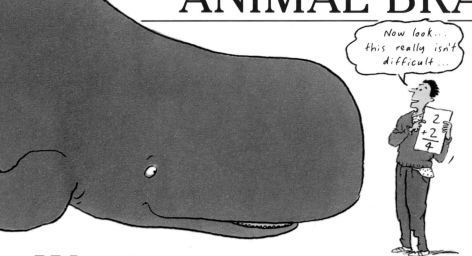

"Now look... this really isn't difficult..."

W hat makes humans more intelligent than any other animal? The answer is, of course, our brains. It is not simply a matter of size. Whales and elephants both have bigger brains than humans, but they would have difficulty taking a simple IQ test!

What counts more is the relative size of our brains. A human brain weighs about 1.35kg (3lbs) and makes up about 2% of human body weight. The world's biggest brain belongs to the sperm whale, which weighs in at 9kg (20lbs) - only 0.02% of body weight. The size of the human cerebrum also sets our brains apart. We have a bigger cerebrum than any other animal.

But although our brains are the most complicated, even the simplest and tiniest animal brain can still do some truly amazing things.

LEARNING

Every animal is born with instincts - things it can do automatically. Many animals survive on instincts alone. But others have the ability to learn skills, using a brain.

THE HONEYBEE

The honeybee has a tiny brain that weighs less than 0.01g (0.0004oz). Yet it has an amazing capacity to learn complex information.

It can learn which flowers give the best pollen and at what times of the day, and all the landmarks within 1 square km (0.4 square mile) of its hive.

"mmm... Yum!"

Honeybees can also pass on information they have learned to other bees. When a bee has found a patch of flowers it goes back to the hive and does a dance to tell the other bees about it.

This dance is called the waggle-dance. It tells other bees how to get to a source of pollen.

NUTCRACKERS

Many animals hide stores of food for the winter. But these are useless if they can't be found again. So these animals have to have good memories. The prize for the best memory goes to a bird called Clark's nutcracker. It stores pine seeds in up to a thousand different places and can find them all again. A human couldn't manage such a feat.

NOT-SO-SLUGGISH?

The seaslug has a brain made up of only 20,000 neurons (a human brain has billions) but it can still learn.

The seaslug is gently touched on its side and doesn't react.

A strong jet of water is then immediately squirted at it. The seaslug recoils at the water jet.

This is repeated several times.

Eventually the seaslug recoils as soon as it is touched. It has learned that one stimulus (a gentle touch) leads to the other (a jet of water).

SOCIABLE APES

Monkeys and apes have brains similar to our own. Like us, they live in large social groups and form complex relationships. Survival does not depend only on getting food and defending themselves. They also need to be able to get along with other monkeys and apes, and to know their status in the group.

A female chimpanzee finds some bananas in a clearing in the forest.

She is about to start eating, when she spots a male approaching.

She hides the bananas, and looks around innocently as if just passing the time of day.

Only when the male turns and walks away into the forest, does she start eating.

But unfortunately for her, the male has stopped behind a tree and is spying on her.

She reluctantly hands the bananas over to him and runs off into the forest.

The female chimp has used her brain to analyze her situation. She identified the male as being more dominant than her, and understood this would mean the bananas would be taken from her. Once spotted though, she knows she has to give them up to avoid being hurt in a fight. Very few animals can manage this kind of thought.

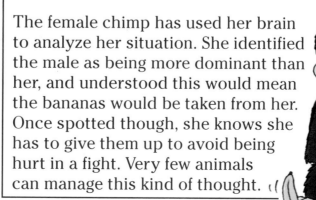

COMPUTER BRAINS

Will the computer ever become more intelligent than the human brain? It's already happened in fiction. In books and films, computers often not only have vast stores of knowledge, but they also have morals, great personalities and can tell jokes. In reality, so little is known about how the brain works, the idea of a computer being able to imitate or better it is unimaginable.

This is Artoo Deetoo, the intelligent computer from the films *Star Wars* and *The Empire Strikes Back.*

INTELLIGENT MACHINES?

In some areas computers are much more efficient than humans. They can analyze huge amounts of data and do long, complicated calculations in a fraction of a second. They can beat all but the very best players at chess. They can help doctors diagnose diseases. Computerized robots can do the work of highly skilled mechanics.

We think of some of these skills as signs of great intelligence in people. But this does not mean that computers are intelligent. In fact, all the computer is doing is following a set of rules which was programmed into it by an intelligent person.

These robots can put together the tiniest parts of cars without taking a break or losing concentration.

Read this list of words.

animal

animal

animal

That was easy, wasn't it? Each word says animal, but in different handwriting. The last word is practically illegible, but because of the words above it, you can guess what it is.

A computer programmed to read handwriting would fail on at least one of these words. This is because computers can follow instructions but are bad at taking a guess.

HUMANIZING COMPUTERS

Although it's false to think of computers as being intelligent, it is true to say that scientists are making computers that behave in more and more human ways. This makes computers easier to use and able to perform functions that are more useful to humans.

One group of people who can benefit enormously from the humanizing of computers is the disabled. The more "human" computers become, the more they will be able to help people.

Computers have given the scientist Stephen Hawking the "freedom" to carry on his work despite being disabled.

There is even a possibility of developing a computer that can act like a part of your nervous system (see page 7). This could give people whose spinal cords have been severed a chance to walk again.

This diagram shows how a computer may one day help someone whose spinal cord is broken to walk.

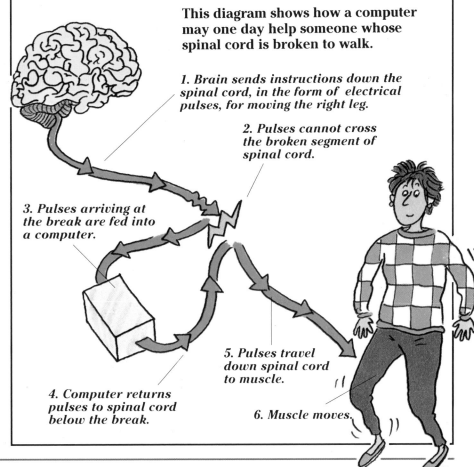

1. Brain sends instructions down the spinal cord, in the form of electrical pulses, for moving the right leg.

2. Pulses cannot cross the broken segment of spinal cord.

3. Pulses arriving at the break are fed into a computer.

4. Computer returns pulses to spinal cord below the break.

5. Pulses travel down spinal cord to muscle.

6. Muscle moves.

BRAINS IN HISTORY

Throughout the ages the brain has been a riddle to scientists. Even today, scientists only understand a fraction of what goes on inside your head.

ANCIENT IDEAS

The Ancient Greeks were some of the world's first scientists. They explored many areas of science, including what happens in the human body.

They had many different theories about where in the body thoughts, feelings and emotions came from.

The poet Homer, who lived about three thousand years ago, thought they came from the lungs.

The great Greek scientist, Aristotle (384-322BC), believed that they came from the heart. Many of us still think love comes from the heart, although we know that this is nonsense according to science.

The first really scientific look at the brain was made in the third century BC, by the Greek scientists Herophilus and Erasistratus.

They were some of the first people to dissect (cut up) animal and human bodies in order to find out about what goes on inside.

Their most important work was the discovery of the nervous system (see page 8). This showed that the brain was in charge of much of what happens in the body.

Galen, doctor to the Roman emperors in the 2nd century AD, continued this study of the brain and nervous system. But, because he did much of his research on animals, not humans, he got some things completely wrong. However, he was still considered the world's brain expert for over a thousand years.

PHRENOLOGY

In Europe and America, from the middle of the 18th to the middle of the 19th century, phrenology was a very popular brain science. Phrenologists thought they could analyze a person's character from the shape and bumps of their skull.

Phrenology was taken so seriously that, for a time, it was used to select people for jobs. There was even a suggestion that children's heads should be shaped to bring out good characteristics, and to suppress bad ones.

They believed the skull was shaped by the structure of the brain beneath it, and that different parts of the brain were responsible for very specific characteristics, skills and talents.

The size of the temples, (the area above the cheekbones), for example, were meant to reveal how musical someone was, while the shape of the base of their skull was meant to show if someone would be a good parent.

LOCALIZATION

The idea that different parts of the brain have different functions is called localization. Phrenology was the silliest of all localization theories. But there were serious scientists in the late 19th century who studied localization. Broca and Wernicke both studied the brains of dead stroke patients and discovered the part of the brain that controlled language.

But it was not really until the 20th century, that the mysteries of what actually happens inside the brain were begun to be resolved. With the arrival of new technology, such as brain scans, better microscopes and advanced brain surgery, doctors and scientists have been able to look closely at the brains of living people.

A patient having a brain scan

As more data is collected, more can be understood about what your brain can do. Much, however, remains a mystery.

TREPANNING

Trepanning was an ancient medical practice, that survived until the Middle Ages. It involved making a small hole in someone's skull. This was meant to release evil spirits that were making the patient insane. It may actually have helped some patients with brain growths, but in most cases it probably did more harm than good.

PUZZLE ANSWERS
Right or Left?
1. d (Right); **2.** 5 (Left); **3.** c
(Right); **4.** Mary (Right)
Taking the test
1. 22; **2.** 3; **3.** The middle shape;
4. 5; **5.** Short; **6.** Bird;
7. Yes:

8. The second piece from the left.
9. 6

ACKNOWLEDGEMENTS
Cover: Eye of Science/Science Photo Library (SPL). Page 2:
Petit Format/J.D. Bauple/SPL. Page 10: Oxford and County
Newspapers. Page 13: *Man and Girl* series of ambiguous
figures - Fisher, G.H. (1967) From "Perception of ambiguous
stimulus materials," Perception and Psychophysics, 2:421-22.
Reprinted by permission of Psychonomic Society, Inc. Page
20: National Library of Medicine/SPL. Page 23: Scan
comparing two brains - U.S. National Institute of Health/SPL;
Scan showing blocked artery - CNRI/SPL. Page 28: Artoo
Deetoo - TM & © Lucasfilm Ltd. (LFL) 1980. All Rights
Reserved. Courtesy of Lucasfilm Ltd. BFI Stills, Posters and
Designs; Robotic welding machine - George Haling/SPL. Page
29: Rex Features Ltd - Assignments. Page 31: BSIP DPA/SPL.